DEMCO

The Library of Author Biographies

Virginia Hamilton

The Library of Author Biographies

VIRGINIA HAMILTON

Deborah A. Marinelli

Published in 2003 by The Rosen Publishing Group, Inc.
29 East 21st Street, New York, NY 10010

Library of Congress Cataloging-in-Publication Data

Marinelli, Deborah A.
Virginia Hamilton / Deborah A. Marinelli.— 1st ed.
    p. cm. — (The library of author biographies)
Summary: Details the life of prominent, award-winning author, Virginia Hamilton, and discusses her work.
Includes bibliographical references (p.) and index.
ISBN 0-8239-3777-1
1. Hamilton, Virginia—Juvenile literature. 2. Authors, American—20th century—Biography—Juvenile literature. 3. African American authors—Biography—Juvenile literature. 4. Children's stories—Authorship—Juvenile literature. 5. African Americans in literature—Juvenile literature. [1. Hamilton, Virginia. 2. Authors, American. 3. African Americans—Biography. 4. Women—Biography.] I.Title. II. Series.
PS3558.A444 Z775 2002
813'.54--dc21

                                        2002011377

Manufactured in the United States of America

Table of Contents

Introduction:
At the Forefront

Virginia Hamilton won every major award given to children's writers. She was the first African American to win the coveted Newbery Medal and the first children's writer to be honored with a MacArthur "genius grant." Her book *M. C. Higgins, the Great* (1974) never went out of print. The *Horn Book Magazine* stated, "In 1974, Virginia Hamilton dazzled the world with her powerful account of a young man's coming of age, trapped between the heritage of his mountain home and his desires for the future. Twenty-five years later, *M. C. Higgins, the Great* remains the only novel ever to win the Newbery Medal, the National Book

Award, and the *Boston Globe/Horn Book Award.*"[1] In 1998, Roberta Trites of Illinois State University wrote of Virginia Hamilton, "[She] is the most important author writing for children in the United States."[2]

Few children's books were written about African American families before Hamilton began her career. In 2000, the critic Michael Strickland wrote, "Hamilton has (helped to fill) the glaring lack of (ethnic) children's literature that existed until recent years."[3] Her work was fresh and personal, without the angry political edge so common in books about African Americans published in the 1960s and 1970s, when most authors focused on racism. Even when she wrote about children with problems, such as Tree, who is burdened with the care of a handicapped brother in *Sweet Whispers, Brother Rush* (a Newbery Honor Book in 1983), something positive shone through. The well-known children's author Katherine Paterson said of *Brother Rush*, "It fairly reaches off the first page to grab you, and once it's got you, it sets you spinning deeper and deeper into the story."[4]

Many of Hamilton's books are, in some way, about the gulf between insiders and outsiders. She asks the same questions over and over again: Who is included? And who is left out? Often, her left-out characters show the greatest growth. They always feel pride in themselves before the book's end.

For her African American characters, race mattered, but it was not necessarily the most important thing. Hamilton invented a phrase, "parallel cultures," that she often referred to when she spoke to groups. Think about railroad tracks, she said: how their parallel lines never come together. Black and white cultures also have the potential to stay far apart. But train tracks change shape at the end of the line; they curve so cars can turn around to go back where they came from. And black and white cultures can change direction to come together, too. Do they always?, she liked to ask. No, but they can.

In fact, they did in Hamilton's private life, for she fell in love with a Jewish New Yorker, an author named Arnold Adoff. They married, lived happily together for more than forty years, and had two talented children: Jaime Levi, who became an author and a musician, and Leigh, who pursued a career as an opera singer.

Though Hamilton was famous and a world traveler, she was also a contented homebody. She loved flowers, and the rich farmland outside her modern redwood home was studded with daffodils, roses, forsythia, and honeysuckle. She enjoyed having fresh-cut blooms in the house all the time and prized her sunroom with its thriving plants. In addition, she and Adoff grew a variety of tomatoes: little cherry ones for snacking, big San Martinos for cooking. Adoff often kept a pot of fresh red sauce simmering on the stove. As the two of them worked on their books, the smell of spices and tomatoes richly blended until dinnertime.

Each morning, Hamilton awoke, fired up her computer, and began writing that day's chapter. Sometimes she took library research days, sifting through local history papers. Some of these were so fragile she had to wear white gloves as she worked. Other times, an ordinary garage sale yielded some knickknack that inspired ideas and images for whatever book she was working on. In her later years, she sometimes hired talented young people to help make sure that facts were checked to her satisfaction.

Hamilton had been writing professionally for more than thirty-five years when, on February 19, 2002, she passed away in Dayton, Ohio. She was sixty-five years old. Friends and readers across the country were unprepared for the news. Although she battled cancer for ten years, only a few people knew that she was ill. Nolan Miller, one of her professors from Antioch College, said, "She was very brave. And she was very down-to-earth. Writers often make a big fuss about what they do. They talk about how hard it is. Virginia never did that. She made it seem easy, which it wasn't."[5]

Her body of work included nearly forty books: biography, mystery, folklore, history, science fiction, and novels. She always wrote from her heart, usually in the voice of a twelve-year-old. It was easy, she said, because she really felt about twelve inside.

Even after her death, Hamilton remained, in the minds of her readers, an impish little girl with a magical grab bag of wonderful tales. To understand how this could be, and why it was so, one must drop back in time nearly 150 years—to her family's first days in Ohio, where her grandfather settled as a young runaway slave.

1 History's Child

On March 12, 1936, Virginia Esther Perry Hamilton was born in Yellow Springs, Ohio, a quiet rural village. During the Civil War years (1861–1865), this area was well-known as a refuge for African Americans who escaped from slavery.

Hamilton's remarkable grandfather, Levi Perry, escaped to freedom as a boy. Virginia Hamilton was named in honor of the state of Virginia, where her grandfather's story began. In 1857, after being spirited away to Ohio by his mother Mary Cloud, a Potawatomi Indian, young Levi was helped by the men and women of the Underground Railroad—a secret network that protected slaves until they crossed a free state's border. Once Levi was safely settled, his mother vanished, never to be heard from again. More than a hundred years would pass before this family story inspired Hamilton's book, *The House of Dies Drear* (1968).

Eventually, Levi Perry bought a farm and married Rhetta Adams, who was part African American and part Cherokee Indian. Levi and Rhetta had ten children together, including a daughter who would grow up to be Virginia Hamilton's mother.

Virginia Hamilton's parents already had four children at home when their youngest daughter was born. Nina was the eldest, followed by Kenneth James (Buster) Jr., Barbara, and William. To better support his growing family, Virginia's father, Kenneth Hamilton Sr., earned a degree from Iowa State Business College. In addition to farming the rich land that had been in his wife's family for almost a century, he managed the food service at Antioch College. He earned extra income by running a gambling establishment.

Hamilton remembered her father as a great reader. He was also a gifted mandolin player, performing on demand for family members and friends at the African Methodist Episcopal

Church. Surviving pictures show a good-looking man with deep, compelling eyes, a strong nose, and laugh lines that border a sensitive mouth. By all accounts, he was multitalented, well-versed in history, social issues, and family lore. When Virginia became famous and spoke of him to newspaper reporters, she often described him as "The Knowledge."

Photographs of Etta Belle Perry Hamilton, Virginia's mother, highlight a graceful nose and chin, lovely dark hair piled on her head, and a single strand of pearls revealing a flair for classic fashion. Hamilton said that her mother was a tiny woman, not even five feet tall, and pleasantly round. Though never a trained writer, she bent language to her will and told wonderful stories.

The Hamilton-Perry family farms—her parents' property and the Perry land that belonged to her mother's relatives—clustered near the National Road, the "old Route 40, which opened the West,"[1] on land the Perrys had held since the late 1880s. Around the time of Virginia's birth, President Franklin Delano Roosevelt and the entire country were still suffering through the Great Depression. Federal job programs were in place across America. They had been created during the Depression to lift families out of poverty, but not that many government jobs were available to Ohioans.

Fortunately, the Hamiltons never went hungry. Etta Belle was a working farm wife who maintained a flock of several hundred leghorn chickens. These were handsome birds with red combs, yellow bills, and bright red wattles that shook when they walked; they made good eating. She also raised exotic Araucana birds with fluffy ear tufts. Their eggs were usually pale blue or green.

Besides chickens, the Hamiltons also raised hogs. This helped Virginia Hamilton write knowledgeably about a pig farmer and his mysterious daughter in her first book, *Zeely*, published in 1967. For produce, they grew corn, melons, cucumbers, and tomatoes. Hamilton wrote in *Horn Book Magazine* that during planting season her father "made the long rows with his hoe, and I'd drop the seeds in a row, spacing them with utmost care and a watchful eye. Then we would cover the seeds with the sweet-scented ground. And look to the sky to let it rain."[2]

Once her seeds sprouted, Virginia helped out by weeding morning glories from the straight rows of vegetables. She said she was paid a penny a row for this chore, not a bad rate for a very young gardener in the early 1940s.

Etta Belle was relaxed about child-rearing, requiring only that her little girl "go to Sunday School, be on the Honor Roll, and come home before dark."[3] Virginia was allowed to ride her red bicycle and to run freely with her cousin, Marleen, who was also her best friend. When the two got together, they were no strangers to mischief.

"One of us got the bright idea to walk the oak crossbeam thirty feet up almost at the top of Uncle Willy's hay barn," Hamilton said. "I no longer recall which one of us had the thought, but I do know that my cousins and I had a serious discussion concerning the proper way to get across that beam, which was all of five or six inches wide. We decided, finally, that the best way to get across without falling was barefoot. The most exciting way would be barefoot and running across. And of course, the most daring, the scariest way had to be barefoot and blindfolded. We accomplished all three and in that order."[4]

Though life was quiet and simple in Yellow Springs, there was a lot of laughter in the family. "I am descended from dirt farmers, eccentric individuals who never failed to see the humor in a

16

monotonous Ohio landscape," she explained. "Any tale was a good tale when told by a relative."[5] Hamilton's parents, aunts, and uncles were born storytellers. "That is the way my family communicated," Hamilton said. "That is how they taught their children. I saw through my mother's eyes, through my grandmother's, my father's and so forth."[6]

"I never tired of hearing the stories of mother and mother's sisters, aunts and cousins. These women took real life and transformed it into something bigger, or funnier, or less frightening than it was."[7]

Etta Belle had a soothing touch that was evident in Virginia's childhood attitude toward race relations. Hamilton encountered bigots in her life on more than one occasion, but she handled them with great maturity. When grown, she said that her early exposure to racism had not been that traumatic.

One such incident she did recall involved the local movie theater. Like most other U.S. states in those days, Ohio permitted theater owners to use a double standard in seating patrons. Whites and blacks were kept apart, and white families were routinely ushered to the better seats. In the 1940s, Virginia "picked berries all morning, then hurried to sell them before dusk to pay for a movie ticket. 'We had to sit in the back,' she recalled, 'but I thought that was wonderful because I could turn up my seat and see over the heads of all the adults.'"[8] It was a remarkably mild point of view for an African American woman who lived through historic civil rights struggles: the August 28, 1963, March on Washington, when 250,000 people protested against racism and Dr. Martin Luther King Jr. made his famous "I Have a Dream" speech; the 1961–1964 Mississippi freedom bus rides to register African American voters in southern states; and the assassination in Memphis, Tennessee, of Martin Luther King, on April 4, 1968.

Her ability to relate in a positive way to all races sprang from having her talent recognized and encouraged not only by a loving family, but also by Yellow Springs villagers on both sides of the color line. In account after account of her childhood, Hamilton described it as pleasant and secure, a lasting testimony to her family's ability to teach her about an imperfect world while protecting her from its worst features. In general, Hamilton thought Yellow Springs was an ideal hometown. In 1981, she said, "The longer I remain in this small village, my time and place in Ohio, the more deeply I comprehend it as the source of all the fiction I create. There is no glamour for me in the sight of distant places, though I enjoy exploring them. My subject matter is the hometown and the hometown's people."[9]

As a young girl, Virginia attended a school where for a long time she was the only African American student. She excelled in reading, spelling, writing, and English, and she won a prize for reading the most books in a year. She made frequent stops at the local library, where she loved to check out armloads of books. There, a library volunteer known as the Story Lady often read aloud to children, and Virginia loved to listen. She also enjoyed the treat of dining now and then at the Antioch College cafeteria, where she could be close to her father as he worked.

In her senior year at Yellow Springs High School, she was popular—a cheerleader and a basketball player. She was also the top graduate in her class. Once, she said, she wrote a school play and somehow persuaded the Yellow Springs football and basketball teams to act in it.

Race struggles may have been played down by the Hamiltons, but they were never forgotten.

Each year, Grandfather Levi Perry retold the story of his escape from Virginia to Ohio, cautioning the young Hamilton children to take care that slavery never happened to them. Though slave days were long past, Grandfather Perry never took his family's freedom for granted.

Hamilton's college-graduate father had a disturbing story of his own to tell. As a young professional, he was once invited to report to a bank where a "suitable" job awaited him. He "arrived dressed in a business suit and was handed a mop and broom. He threw both mop and broom 'the length of the establishment and turned on his heel, never to return.'"[10] The painful experiences of her father and grandfather inspired Hamilton to write what she called "liberation literature, stories of unsung and well-known individuals who, against great odds, pursued their freedom."[11] Included was *Anthony Burns: The Defeat and Triumph of a Fugitive Slave* (1988), her account of the last fugitive from slavery to be taken back into bondage from the state of Massachusetts.

Usually, though, Hamilton's characters did not dwell on whatever held them back. Rather, they celebrated the small, everyday pleasures of family and school life. It was as if Hamilton were saying that her young characters deserved a few happy, innocent years before they took on all of the world's pain. Part of the great power of her novels, something that set her apart, was her rare ability to present young people not as adults saw them, but as they saw each other. Their delight in magic and secrets, in neighborhood mysteries, in teasing between sisters and brothers, was a mirror image of the author's happy and secure upbringing.

Hamilton called her family's story sessions "tellings," and she often tested the promise of a new book by first telling its story to a small group of listeners. For reporter Nancy Gilson of the *Columbus Dispatch*, Hamilton recalled a "tell" of an earlier year when Yellow Springs flooded and a mass of frogs suddenly appeared everywhere. She used this image in her book *Plain City* (1993), the story of a bright twelve-year-old loner, Bulaire, who struggled to come to terms with the past and her troubled father.

The frog scene amused readers, who began to send her frog figurines and frog art that grew into a large collection she featured on her Web site. She also told Gilson that, to her young eyes, especially at dusk, silos on neighboring farms closely resembled spaceships that were about to take off. Her active imagination helped her write a rare example of African American science fiction, the "Justice" series, featuring Justice, a young girl with telepathic and telekinetic powers, and her twin brothers Thomas and Levi. *Justice and Her Brothers* (1978), *Dustland* (1980), and *The Gathering* (1981) chronicled their adventures.

As a young girl, Virginia enjoyed words. Early on in school, she read and memorized poetry, often reciting in class. Virginia and her classmates also read aloud frequently. Encouraged to believe that language and reading were play, that tale-telling was the most fun and social part of life, and that good stories were hers for the asking, she seemed fated to become an author. Hamilton said that writers like herself have to work through all sorts of different situations—that they are always writing, even when not physically doing so. For Hamilton, the world was a story.

Virginia had gotten lost in the world of her imagination as far back as she could remember. "My Aunt Betty said when I went down the street I looked like a little fairy," she said. "I was very thin, kind of wide-eyed, dreamy. I always kept my own counsel. I was born to live within my mind, to have thoughts and dreams more vivid to me than any daylight."[12] Growing up, she eagerly made her way through a home library that heavily featured classic works. She said she didn't then realize how unusual it was for a man like her father to have such books. In the seventh grade, she began to write creatively, but it wasn't yet a burning passion. At the time, she considered writing another activity to be balanced with track and cheerleading.

Despite being the top high school graduate, Virginia did not know if she could attend college right away. The scholarship that should have gone to her as the top scholar in her class went instead to a white student. Instead of giving up, though, Virginia approached Jesse Triechler, the wife of Paul Triechler, theater professor at Antioch College in Yellow Springs—the same campus where Virginia's father managed food services. Jesse and Paul were aware of Virginia's talent. They also knew that she had written and produced a high school play. Convinced that Virginia deserved a break, Jesse worked the phones until she found sponsorship in New York for an Antioch College scholarship. Not only would the scholarship package pay for Virginia's tuition, it would also cover room and board in the college dormitory.

Antioch had always been in the forefront of American colleges. It was the first campus in the United States to admit men and women on an equal basis, and it attracted top students who cared about the arts and social justice. Virginia realized she had been given the opportunity of a lifetime. In short order, she thanked the Triechlers, prepared to enroll, and decided to declare creative writing as her college major.

2 College and the Real World

As a student living at home with her parents, Hamilton had read the *Saturday Evening Post*, the *New Yorker*, the *Crisis*, and the NAACP (National Association for the Advancement of Colored People) journal edited by W. E. B. DuBois, an early civil rights leader she would write a book about in 1972. She enjoyed reading great writers such as Eudora Welty, winner of the Pulitzer Prize for her novel *The Optimist's Daughter* (1973); Flannery O'Connor, winner of the National Book Award for her *Complete Short Stories* (1972); Californian Jack London, best known for his Alaska stories and *The Call of the Wild* (1903); and Richard Wright, most famous for his books *Black Boy* (1945) and

Native Son (1940). For the rest of Hamilton's life, she passionately loved the prose of the great southern writer William Faulkner, who won both the 1950 Nobel Prize for Literature and the 1955 Pulitzer Prize. Having read through the greatest voices in literature, she was ready to learn the nuts-and-bolts lessons she would need to publish her own work in the future.

As small as Antioch College was, it was home to a renowned writing teacher, Nolan Miller. During Miller's long and interesting career, he befriended Anne Sexton, Tillie Olsen, and many other important authors. Miller's eye for new talent was sharp. Even before Virginia Hamilton arrived on campus, he read one of her writing samples and thought at once that she was the real thing.

Everyone who applied to the college had to submit an essay outlining their future plans. Fifty years after Hamilton turned hers in, Nolan Miller still remembered it. He recalled getting very excited by her words, for she already had an uncommon gift.

Miller's teaching methods were unique. He liked to say, "I don't teach writing. I teach students."[1] He understood that creative writing was very different from, for example, mathematics, where each problem has one right answer. Each of his writing students had different strengths. Some were natural poets, some wrote good short stories, and others liked to write nonfiction. Miller was able to give each student plenty of attention, because there were never more than twelve in his class at any one time. In Hamilton, he saw not just a talented student, but also a writer who refused to copy others. A lot of Miller's students were imitating Ernest Hemingway in those days, but Hamilton never did. "She was always interested in reading, in the life of the mind," Miller said. "She had a great fascination for the world of the past."[2]

Antioch students were required to be a part of campus government, to help design their own study programs, and to gain on-the-job experience. The summer after her freshman year, Hamilton signed up for a required work-study experience at the Irene Kaufmann Settlement House, a service center for the poor in Pittsburgh. When she returned to Yellow Springs in the fall, she wrote a long account of what it had been like for her there. Miller read it and was deeply moved by her account. He told her, in no uncertain terms, "You are a writer."[3] A later work-study project at the Urban League in

New York City, which was founded to help minorities prosper and move into leadership roles, would take Hamilton to the city where she knew many famous writers lived.

Someone else who got to see Hamilton's early writing at Antioch was Janet Schulman, who would become vice president and editor-at-large of Random House Children's Books. Schulman, a literature major, transferred to Antioch from Pennsylvania State University in 1953. Her second year in Yellow Springs, she lived directly across the hall from Hamilton and they got to know each other well. "Her roommate and my roommate were friends; we were a kind of foursome," Schulman recalled. "Virginia frequently read to me what she had written for Nolan Miller's class."

In those days, Hamilton's appearance was quite exotic. "She weighed 97 pounds and I guess she was about 5 feet 8," Janet Schulman said. "She was a bit like her character Zeely, very statuesque and elegant and a little mysterious. I don't remember if she ever actually wrote poetry but her prose was very poetic and haunting, hard to parse, and very different from most creative writing majors of that time."[4]

As an African American student in the nearly all-white college, Hamilton excited a certain amount of interest. Nolan Miller remembered no racial barriers in Yellow Springs, but only a handful of black Antiochians had enrolled before Hamilton. This had nothing to do with college policy, though. With a student body of about 1,000 (the college now has more than 4,000 students), Antioch College welcomed minority students in its preparatory academy as early as 1855; the college graduated its first African American student in the 1880s.

Hamilton may have been surprised that her out-of-town classmates viewed Yellow Springs as a vital community of thinkers that provided plenty of fun and interesting activities. The relationship between locals and students was marked by mutual respect, not surprising because Yellow Springs natives included professionals and free thinkers who cared what was happening in the rest of the country and the world. Townspeople tended to be politically active and appreciated the arts.

For her Antioch drama teacher, Paul Triechler, Hamilton drafted a short story about a 6' 6" tall striking African American woman who lived in the country and raised pigs, but who seemed to have a mysterious, perhaps even a royal, aura about her. Hamilton later said that her inspiration came from a photograph she saw of an exotic Watusi woman in *Life* magazine. One day, Janet Schulman listened to her friend's unusual story, then entitled "The West Field," and mentally filed it away. A decade later, Schulman would find herself in a unique position to remind Hamilton of this piece of writing—an act that would have profound repercussions.

In 1956, Hamilton decided to transfer to Ohio State University. It was time to get out of town and learn something more about life. Her new home, Columbus—Ohio's state capital—then had a population of 446,227. Columbus was just over an hour's drive from her family, so Hamilton would be able to visit them when she got homesick.

Ohio State University students referred to themselves as "buckeyes,"[5] which were shiny dark brown nuts with lighter tan patches resembling the eyes of a deer. Buckeyes flourished locally and were known for their grit. They grew where others could not and adapted to their circumstances with ease—something Hamilton did throughout her life.

Virginia Hamilton's parents probably hoped that Columbus would satisfy their youngest daughter's appetite for change, but her dreams of

Manhattan, fueled by her work-study job with the Urban League, refused to go away. After an OSU teacher suggested that she go directly to New York to try to publish her work, Hamilton finally felt that she was ready to consider it seriously. However, the decision to leave her family behind was a difficult one. She was also concerned about what such a move would cost. In 1996, she told Claudia Feldman of the *Houston Chronicle* that she didn't graduate from either college she attended because she simply didn't have enough money to pay for all her classes. For a time, she went back and forth from Columbus to New York.

Eventually, she settled permanently in New York, and almost at once she began one of the most exciting and growth-filled periods of her life. She told an audience of booksellers that she was told a great, gold pot was waiting for her, but no rockets exploded in the air on her arrival. In time, though, she learned about city life and survival. She said she also learned to write the best way—by living.

In those days, Hamilton thought of herself as a young New York sophisticate. "I affected a dark beret, trench coat, velvet slacks, and a cigarette holder. It was a time of cool jazz and 'shades' worn at night. One did not sit at the Five Spot Cafe in Manhattan; one lounged artfully, Joyce's *Dubliners* tucked under the arm. One did not applaud the musicians after a good set or tune; one snapped one's fingers; one was cool; one rarely spoke; but instead delicately touched a shoulder, or fingertips to other fingertips, or to one's lips in a sweet blown kiss goodbye."[6] The drug problems that would plague New York in the sixties, seventies, and eighties were not yet a threat. It was safe and a great deal of fun to walk around at night, watching the neighbors, listening to folk music and jazz, and looking in the windows of shops.

To make enough money to eat and pay her rent, Hamilton got jobs as a cost accountant and as a receptionist at the Cooper Union Gallery. She sometimes felt wistful about working in offices when she felt she needed to be writing. The neighborhood she moved into, Manhattan's East Village, had been a community of poor immigrants, but by the late fifties, writers and artists from the West Village had begun to trickle in, lured by cheap rents and affordable cafés and clubs. Hamilton said that her first apartment there, which didn't even have a radiator, "cost just $48 per month."[7]

East Village bookstores were among the best in the city, and a number of them specialized in used books. Even on a strict budget, Hamilton could afford a few treasures for her library. She also enjoyed an occasional movie out. Her neighbors were a vibrant mix of races, nationalities, and religions. Part of her East Village experience was hearing many different languages and enjoying the exotic smells of cooking from immigrant kitchens. New York City, the home of Malcolm X, was a center of early civil rights activity. Hamilton told interviewer Nina Mikkelsen that she began writing, "at the time of 'Black is Beautiful' on through black power and throughout the Malcolm X time and all the disasters that befell this country."[8]

If New York publishers failed to welcome her with open arms and big checks in her early career, they were at least encouraging. Hamilton told writer Gale McDowell that the *New Yorker* had sent her promising rejection letters during that time. Hoping to break through and see her words in print, she signed up for a class at the New School for Social Research, which welcomed those hoping to become writers, photographers, playwrights, and poets.

At the New School, Hamilton once again found a talented and well-connected teacher. His name was Hiram Hayden, and he was considered a top New York editor—he had recently been invited to join a publishing house called Atheneum as a third partner. When Hamilton registered for "Studies in Writing the Novel," she knew that this influential man was actively scouting for future literary stars. At the time, Hamilton was working on a novel for adults she called *Mayo*. She brought her draft to class, and to her delight, Hayden seemed interested in it. For a long time, he held out hope that *Mayo* would be published by Atheneum. Hamilton revised her novel over and over again. In the end, her teacher regretfully turned the book down. He told a deeply disappointed Hamilton that although he wanted to buy it, his two partners in the new company refused to go along.

Virginia Hamilton could not have known it then, but whatever pain and humiliation she felt after the rejection would be very short-lived. Before long, everything in her life would be different. Good fortune was about to come her way.

3 Life Partner and Life Work

In the late 1950s, Virginia Hamilton kept hearing from her friends that a man named Arnold Adoff was someone she would like. He was a poet and a writer who paid his West Village rent by substitute-teaching in New York City schools. On the side, he managed a thirty-five-year-old African American jazz man named Charles Mingus, who was a master bassist and also played piano, composed music, led a band, and founded his own music publishing company. When he died in 1979, Mingus was praised as one of America's greatest musicians. When Adoff managed him, though, he was an emerging artist who sometimes had trouble finding jobs.

Arnold Adoff, the son of Aaron and Rebecca Adoff, was Jewish and from the East Bronx. He was a graduate of New York's prestigious Stuyvesant High School, which had an all-boy student body in those days. Stuyvesant was famously strong in math, science, and the technologies; two Nobel Prize winners and many notable scientists graduated from there. Because Adoff was not a science or math whiz, he sometimes felt a little out of place, but he liked playing trombone in the high school band. Adoff's experience at Stuyvesant opened him to the world outside his small Jewish neighborhood. He got to meet people of different races and religions and economic and cultural backgrounds.

After high school, Adoff earned a bachelor of arts degree in history and government from City College. In the spring of 1958, he spent six months in the army. When he got out, he rented an apartment in the West Village. This was an exciting time in New York. At local clubs, you could hear Bob Dylan before he became a famous folk singer, and jazz greats such as Charlie Parker and Miles Davis played in small neighborhood clubs.

In the midst of this nonstop neighborhood celebration, Arnold Adoff would catch a glimpse of Virginia Hamilton, or she would notice him.

At a Christmas party in 1958, their paths crossed again. This time, Hamilton talked with Adoff. It was an interesting situation. A stranger sizing up the African American-Jewish couple would have first noticed their differences, and other contrasts were more than skin deep. Hamilton grew up in the country, Adoff in the city. However, their shared love of reading, music, adventure, and the fact that Hamilton was writing a first novel, *Mayo*, and that Adoff was a poet, gave them much in common. When the party finally ended, they reluctantly parted.

At three o'clock in the morning, Adoff worked up his nerve, picked up the phone, called Hamilton, and started to read his poetry to her. He had written seriously for years. After he shared his poetry with her, their talk drifted into other areas. It was during that long, late-night conversation that they began to fall in love.

Friends happily supported the match, and on Saturday, March 19, 1960, at eight o'clock in the morning, Virginia Hamilton and Arnold Adoff were married in New York City's Municipal Building. In years to come, Hamilton's memory was that their wedding day was sunny; Adoff remembered it as being rainy. Janet Schulman and her husband, Lester, who had moved to New York City in 1960, were their witnesses for the civil ceremony.

Though the day was happy and exciting, the bride and groom knew that their marriage would not be lawful in a number of states. In 1960, the Current Population Survey reported only 51,000 interracial marriages in the entire United States; now there are at least half a million. ". . . Even in the most enlightened areas, mixed-race couples . . . [had a hard time]. Clerks refused to issue marriage licenses to mixed couples, and ministers often wouldn't marry them."[1] Impossible as it seems today, at the time of Hamilton and Adoff's wedding, the penalty for such marriages in Washington, D.C., was one to five years in prison. Not until 1967 were laws against interracial marriage finally thrown out in Virginia and fifteen other states.

The couple did not allow the biased racial attitudes of others to spoil their happiness. They began a long and exciting trip overseas, where Europeans welcomed them warmly. After stays in Spain and Morocco, they returned to New York where Adoff accepted a job as a teacher and in his off hours, took classes at

Columbia University, New York University, and Connecticut College. Both Hamilton and Adoff wanted to work full-time on their book projects. To try to make it happen, they agreed to a five-year plan. Hamilton said, "I would take the first five years to find out if I could become a published author. Arnold would take the second five years, only if and when I failed at the first. It turned out he taught school while I stayed home polishing my prose."[2]

Hamilton still felt let down by *Mayo* and wondered what her next move should be. Then, one day, Janet Schulman—who by then had landed a job in marketing for Macmillan's Children's Books—remembered the unusual story that Hamilton had written at Antioch. Perhaps this could be rewritten as a children's book, she suggested.

Hamilton asked her what a children's book was. She knew that such books existed, but she had never paid attention to what made them different from the books adults read. With help from Schulman, she was able to get Dick Jackson, then the second-ranking editor in Macmillan's children's division, to read her work. He recalled:

> Janet Schulman sent me a pile of pages. They were still a story, not yet a novel . . . I loved the

story and thought there was much in it that warranted development and expansion. Some writer quoted me as saying. "There's a chapter between these two sentences," which was a good way to put it, I thought.

Virginia and I were about the same age. She used to say "Jackson taught me how to write novels." What she really meant, I think, was that I was an excellent listener. We both lived in the same neighborhood on the West Side, and we talked about that book around her kitchen table.[3]

On the promise of Hamilton's ability to complete her strong story, Dick Jackson bought the book (which at that time was called *Geeder and Toe-boy*) for Macmillan before it was finished. She was still working on the book when, in 1965, the Adoffs traveled to Europe for another prolonged stay. "She would send me chunks of that book from Europe," Dick Jackson recalled. "Some text and some tape recordings. Then months would go by and I wouldn't hear a thing. Slowly and surely, though, *Zeely* developed as it currently is."[4]

Geeder and Toe-boy was finally published as *Zeely* in 1967. In the book, Elizabeth, or "Geeder," is in awe of an immensely tall woman, whom she imagines to be a royal Watusi. Written in Elizabeth's sweet but mischievous voice, the story is tender and scary, exotic and familiar all at once. The problems set before the reader are not overly fantastic. They are like the problems people struggle with in real life. The book touched the hearts of children and impressed the critics.

At last, Hamilton could hold a book she had written in her hands and enjoy the sight of her name on the cover. It had been many years since she began working to publish her writing, but because she set out on her career path so early, she achieved her dream by the age of thirty-one. Meanwhile, Hamilton and Adoff became the parents of a daughter, Leigh, and a son, Jaime Levi. Both children grew up to work in the entertainment business, where wise performers keep age a closely held secret. Because of this, the family has never confirmed the children's exact birth dates. It is a matter of public record, though, that Hamilton dedicated *Zeely* to her daughter (and to Leigh's grandmother, Etta) in 1967.

Over time, it became obvious that the publication of this book was an important event. Sales were good, and *Zeely* was recognized as an American Library Association Notable Book, a tremendous honor for a first time author. There is no question that *Zeely* got a boost from the United States's growing interest in ethnic stories; but the book and its characters were so completely one-of-a-kind that it would have succeeded even if it hadn't been published at the right moment in history. It was translated into several foreign languages and is still in print nearly four decades later. Critics have called it a modern-day classic.

Susan Hirschman at Macmillan (who took over as Hamilton's editor when Dick Jackson left the company in 1966) was ready to publish another Virginia Hamilton book. She was confident that her new author would be successful with future titles. For this next book, Hamilton decided she would go far back in time and place for inspiration, all the way to her Grandfather Levi's escape from slavery, and to her family's rich farmlands in Ohio's Yellow Springs.

4 An Honored Writer Returns to Her Home

The year Virginia Hamilton began writing her second book, 1968, was a time of sorrow for the United States. On April 4, Martin Luther King Jr., who led black Americans through Mississippi freedom fights, struggles to open the all-white Birmingham schools, and the historic March on Washington, was assassinated on the balcony of the Motel Lorraine in Memphis, Tennessee. His murder sent shock waves through the country. On June 5, just two months later, Robert F. Kennedy, a senator from New York deeply committed to civil rights, was assassinated at the

Ambassador Hotel in Los Angeles. He had hoped to follow President John F. Kennedy, his brother, into the White House.

Many people observed these events and feared that the United States had entered a violent era of casual killings. The country had changed, and so had New York. Gone were the mellow, music-enlivened streets of the fifties. Crime statistics skyrocketed. Meanwhile, Hamilton's career seemed to be moving in a promising direction, and Adoff, too, had landed a book contract. It began to look as if their hard work to become full-time writers would pay off, enabling them to live anywhere they wished.

Etta Hamilton was getting older, and Virginia wanted to go back to Yellow Springs to be closer to her mother. She was homesick anyway. To her editors, Virginia Hamilton wrote, "In my generation, many women left the safety of home and tradition. I left my small Ohio town to seek my fortune and become a writer in the big city, New York. Years later, I returned. I had found my way (publishing!) and I could come home again. My community welcomed me with open arms. I love my hometown . . . I believe there is nothing quite like an Ohio sunset. On the edge of this town, mornings can be immensely quiet, until the birds start in with their singing. All of it feeds my heart and my mind, and my writing."[1]

Etta Hamilton sold the last two acres of the family farm to Virginia and Arnold. The Adoffs then built their permanent home, a handsome modern structure of redwood with enormous windows that let in the light and the spectacle of nature. "Here on this land is the best place for me to write," Hamilton said. "I have generations of memories. All of it feeds my heart and mind."[2] In the deep peace of the country, Hamilton and Adoff pulled out their Olivetti typewriters and began their joint life work in earnest. Hamilton began calling them "a two-Olivetti family."[3]

When Hamilton was working on a new project, she almost never worked with an outline. Her method was more free-flowing. As the story that became her second book took shape, her grandfather's tale about the Underground Railroad overtook her writer's vision. Once again, her book would be written for children. Now, however, it would be a mystery, a puzzle with linked parts. The main storyline would take place in the present day, but historic events would also figure importantly. The plot would entertain young readers with surprises and suspense at the same time it taught them about the Underground Railroad and African American history. She titled her new book *The House of Dies Drear*.

As Hamilton told her story, Dies Drear was an abolitionist who used his house as a station on the Underground Railroad. In the modern day, young Thomas Small and his family move into Drear's old place, which has been deserted for quite a while. It contains secret tunnels, passages, and hiding places. Strange things seem to happen there. Mr. Pluto, whose home is a cave inspired by the limestone caverns of Ohio, provides intriguing twists in a quirky featured role.

In *Zeely*, Hamilton had created a very true-to-life atmosphere. Kent State University professor Marilyn Apseloff noted that the pump room that was described in that book was based on a real room owned by Hamilton's Uncle Willie. Most of the other interior settings were based on her Uncle Lee's house. The farm chores in the book were exactly the same as those Virginia Hamilton's family performed on their family farms.

With *Dies Drear*, Hamilton drew from her knowledge of rural life. She was in new territory, however, in plotting a juvenile mystery. Mystery writing is such a specialized craft that most mystery authors never write anything else. It was a real challenge for Hamilton to think up enough twists and turns to keep her tale surprising, but she succeeded.

Macmillan published *The House of Dies Drear* in 1968 and Hamilton prepared herself for the new reviews. She needn't have worried. The book was not only a commercial success, it also received good critical notice as well, winning the Mystery Writers of America's Edgar Allan Poe Award for Best Juvenile Mystery in 1969. Hamilton said this award meant a lot to her, because Edgar Allan Poe was one of the authors her father had collected in his library.

With two published books under her belt in just two years, both of them prize-winning, Hamilton was now confident of her ability to craft a spellbinding story. Despite the force she had built in her career, however, and the fact that *Zeely* had been named an American

Library Association Notable Book, it still seemed that the door to the ultimate prize in children's literature might be closed to her.

The Newbery Medal, established in 1921, honors the most distinguished children's book published the previous year, and is awarded by the American Library Association. Named for John Newbery, a British publisher and bookseller of the eighteenth century, it is the best-known juvenile award in the country. Practically every library in the United States has a collection of gold-embossed Newbery Medal books in its children's department. At the time, Hamilton published *Zeely* and *The House of Dies Drear*, no African American author had ever won the coveted medal.

Others in the book world noticed the situation. In 1969, librarians Glyndon Greer and Mabel McKissack were both attending the annual conference of the American Library Association in Atlantic City, New Jersey. The women stood in line at the booth of publisher John Carroll, hoping to bring home one of his souvenir posters of Martin Luther King Jr. As they waited, they chatted about the fact that African American writers had not been honored for their work in children's literature. John Carroll, overhearing, asked why the two women didn't start such an award themselves.

That chance remark led to the creation of the Coretta Scott King Award. Four other librarians—Harriet Brown, Beatrice James, Roger McDonough, and Ella Gaines Yates— joined Glyndon Greer and Mabel McKissack in establishing a prize that would honor the widow of Dr. King and would give talented African American children's writers the recognition they deserved. The first Coretta Scott King Award, honoring an African American author's outstanding contribution toward promoting a better understanding and appreciation of the culture, did not go to Virginia Hamilton, but to Lillie Patterson for her 1970 biography *Martin Luther King, Jr.: Man of Peace*.

In the future, however, Hamilton would win in 1983 for *Sweet Whispers, Brother Rush*. The *Ingram Journal* pointed out that *Brother Rush* was a *School Library Journal*-starred book and stated that this was Virginia Hamilton at her best. In 1986, Hamilton won the Coretta Scott King Award again for *The People Could Fly: American Black Folktales*. *School Library Journal* said that this collection of twenty-four African American folk tales—including animal tales, supernatural tales, and slave tales of freedom—were beautifully readable.

In 1996, Hamilton won a final time for *Her Stories: African American Folktales, Fairy Tales, and True Tales*—a collection of nineteen tales about African American females. *Booklist*'s review of *Her Stories* praised Hamilton's storytelling as being dramatic and direct.

For Hamilton's next book for Macmillan, she was not content to copy a previously successful formula. With its dreamy use of make-believe, *Zeely* became a classic story; but *The House of Dies Drear* was even better in terms of plotting and atmosphere. Quite a few readers and critics expected that Hamilton would choose to write another mystery or at least a children's tale with mysterious elements, because she'd had great success with that kind of writing, but once more she struck out in a fresh direction. When describing the process of beginning a new tale, she told Marilyn Apseloff, "The first ninety pages of any novel that I do are crucial to the rest of the book, It's either going to make it or not. After those ninety pages, I know."[4]

In *The Time-Ago Stories of Jadhu* (1969), Hamilton drew from the ancient style of oral historians who memorized tales and passed them along to a tribe's young people. A favorite subject of early storytellers was the trickster, a prankster who stays just one step ahead of trouble in a variety of funny ways. In different cultures, there are trickster stories about coyotes, ravens, and sometimes even spiders. Hamilton's trickster, Jadhu, is a shape-shifter who travels through the mountains and woods outwitting the animals as he goes along.

Hamilton's next book, *The Planet of Junior Brown*, was published in 1971. This time, she created a memorable friendship between two eighth-grade boys. "One is a neurotic musical prodigy, Junior Brown. The other, Buddy Clark, is a homeless child of the streets. It is Buddy who takes on the responsibility of helping his isolated friend survive."[5] In 1972, Hamilton published a young adult biography of W. E. B. DuBois, the great editor and civil rights activist whom her father held in such high regard. And in 1973, she returned once more to trickster-lore in *Time-Ago Lost: More Tales of Jahdu*. Both books were published by Macmillan and edited by Susan Hirschman.

In 1974, Hamilton wrote a book many believed was her best yet: *M. C. Higgins, the Great*, again published with Macmillan. Some critics reacted as if *M. C.* were an overnight success, but Hamilton was the author of eight books—nine, counting her unpublished adult novel *Mayo*. Her climb had been steady and deliberate. She was a polished researcher and writer who had paid her dues, not a newcomer to the profession.

Mayo Cornelius Higgins had lived at the foot of his family's mountain ever since his great-grandmother Sarah arrived there as a runaway slave. When his home is threatened by strip mining, it takes two strangers to help him save his beloved mountain. Hamilton dedicated this book to Susan Hirschman, her editor since *Zeely* was still a sheaf of unpublished papers. *M. C.*'s appealing characters, social issues, and masterful construction impressed critics and readers alike. In 1975, a year after *M. C*'s publication, Hamilton finally became the first African American writer to win the Newbery Award, the highest honor in children's publishing. She received the good news in a phone call at 3:00 AM.

Hamilton had become accustomed to praise, but the Newbery Medal was different and special. "Every month, libraries across the country have an evaluation of children's books that come into them from publishing houses," she explained. "They go through a criteria they set up, depending on the library and the library system, what is good, what is needed, what is artistic. When it comes to selecting the Newbery Award, the book is supposed to meet standards of excellence as far as language and ideas. There is a committee of 23. The voting system is very complicated for the Newbery. Sometimes it goes on for 12 to 24 hours. They must vote and vote and vote until they have a certain type of majority, so to win the John Newbery Award is very difficult and the book has to be fairly good to win it."[6]

This was a splendid development that seemed to prove that Virginia Hamilton had made all the right choices. Her happy and stable life with Arnold Adoff and their children, the decision to come home to Yellow Springs to live quietly, her calculated gamble to bypass traditional jobs to focus single-mindedly on a riskier writer's life—it all paid off. She had broken a major barrier for writers of her race and rose to the top of her distinguished profession. And all of this she did before she was forty years old.

5 First Among Children's Writers

F ew writers climb to the top and stay there, but Virginia Hamilton managed to do just that. After she swept the Newbery Medal, the *Boston Globe/Horn Book* Award, and the National Book Award in 1974–1975, her name was known in every library, bookstore, and school in America. The way her young characters spoke drew special praise from critics. In the past, speech patterns of older or less well-educated African Americans were represented by ugly misspellings. Hamilton, who had a keen ear for voices, put an end to this. She sometimes dropped a word or a word ending, but these small shifts resulted in truer renderings of the African American voice. Hamilton's dialogue was so natural sounding, in fact, that it took time for reviewers to notice and comment on the important breakthrough she had made.

After the mid-seventies, bookselling changed greatly. Before then, children's book authors sold mostly to school and public libraries. Around the time Virginia began to enjoy success as a best-selling author, the popularity of paperback publishing soared. Books became very affordable, even for children with limited spending money. School book clubs grew popular, creating hundreds of thousands of additional sales for authors.

Hamilton's vivid imagination, her love of history, her playfulness with words—none of these would have mattered, had she not put in many hours of hard work. The price of such effort, day after day, was high. But finishing a new book made it all seem worthwhile. She wrote as steadily as any author in America, completing at least a book a year. "Novel writing was my first love," Hamilton wrote for her Web site in the essay "Planting Seeds." "I am not sure it remains so. Fiction is totally demanding in the sacrifice of energy, and of a set of mind. It is exhaustive, strange work that finally does not satisfy. But a writer doesn't make novels just for the need of satisfaction. She searches for perfection in writing fiction . . . What is this? Who are these people? What is going on here? How to describe the movement of the shoulders, the arms? I never want to finish a novel, a grand scheme. And once I do, I try to write it over again and again, until Authority—the editor—takes it, snatches it away from me."[1]

Don Wallis, editor of the *Yellow Springs News* and a friend of Hamilton and Adoff, recalled, "One evening a few years ago, after dinner at her house, Virginia showed me the room where she wrote her books. Down the hall was Arnold's room where he wrote his poems. Virginia remarked, matter-of-factly, that the two of them wrote all day, every day, and that often she wrote far into the night. She would write that night, she said, after her dinner guests went home."[2]

Those who knew Hamilton best understood that she and Adoff were a team. Aside from his own writing (several of his books were named ALA Notable Books for Children), Adoff sold publishing rights to both his own and Hamilton's work (in other words, he was their literary agent), and he ran the family business, which permitted Hamilton to keep her mind on writing stories.

After Hamilton won the Newbery Medal, she was once again faced with the choice about whether to stay at Macmillan, where she had published all of her children's fiction, or to follow a gifted editor someplace else. The issue had first arisen when Dick Jackson left Macmillan before *Zeely* was published in 1967. In 1974, the editor who replaced him, Susan Hirschman, was ready to be her own boss. She founded Greenwillow Press, and Hamilton wrote several books for the new publishing house.

Hamilton published some important books at Greenwillow, which later became an imprint of HarperCollins Publishers: *Jadhu* (1980), *Willie Bea and the Time the Martians Landed* (1983), and *The Conclusion of the Dies Drear Chronicle* (1987). However, Hamilton did not limit herself to one publisher. *The Magical Adventures of Pretty Pearl* (1983), the book Hamilton said was her most feminist—the story of a god-child who comes down from her home on Mount Kenya to live among humans—was sold to Harper & Row (now HarperCollins Publishers). She also sold books to other publishers: Philomel, Harcourt, Putnam, and Knopf in the 1980s. The days when one author wrote for just one publisher were over, a change that began when editors themselves began switching jobs.

Hamilton's contracts with Knopf meant a lot to her, as this house published many of the classic books her father had collected. In 1985, Knopf published *The People Could Fly: American Black Folktales*, which won the Coretta Scott King Award, was a *Booklist* Editor's Choice, and was a National Council of Teachers of English (NCTE) Award Book. The word order of this title was intentional. Hamilton's editors wanted her to use Black American Folktales, but she argued that her people were American first and black second. *Anthony Burns: The Defeat and Triumph of a Fugitive Slave* followed in 1988. This was a true and very painful account of a slave's years of freedom and his eventual recapture. It won the *Boston Globe/Horn Book* Award for Nonfiction, the Jane Addams Children's Book Award, the ALA Best Book for Young Adults citation, and many other honors.

If writing absorbed most of her day, her family life took up every remaining hour. After her father's death, Hamilton helped with the care of her elderly mother. Leigh and Jaime were growing into young adults, and to Hamilton and Adoff's delight, both were showing signs of musical talent. Back in her early New York days, Hamilton had tried singing in nightclubs for a while. Now it was obvious that Leigh had inherited her mother's singing talent and could develop it to a professional level. Her soprano voice was so fine, in fact, that she was already considering a career in opera. Female opera singers were often overweight—they used to believe they had to be, to strengthen their voices. Leigh was unusual because her big voice came in a small package. Because she was slender and attractive, and could project well, she had a real chance of succeeding in the competitive world of opera.

Jaime was an instrumental musician who was on his way to organizing his own band. He liked the creativity of making music that was uniquely his own and thought he would enjoy live performing. Both he and his sister looked forward to pursuing their musical dreams in New York, where their parents began their own creative lives.

Sometimes, bookwriting was a lonely and frustrating business. As much as Hamilton loved to lose herself in her work, she also enjoyed visiting with people, particularly those who were young and talented. In 1984, Kent State University began an annual lecture given in her honor. Over the years, this grew into the full-blown Virginia Hamilton Conference, a nationally renowned meeting for children's writers and those who study them. As the nineties approached, Hamilton worked with graduate students as a distinguished visiting professor at Queens College in New York. She was a distinguished visiting professor at Ohio State University in Columbus, her alma mater, as well. She loved teaching and connected easily with students of all ages. Time in the classroom gave her the chance to mix, mingle, and pass her knowledge on to the next generation.

Don Wallis, author of *All We Had Was Each Other* (1988), a history of the African American community in Yellow Springs, remembered Virginia Hamilton as a fabulous teacher, never too busy to help a local high school student. He said that she "listened with rapt [careful] attention as the students read their own writings—works in progress: unfinished stories, first drafts of poems. Then she would give her response to their work, speaking as seriously and intently as if she were critiquing the work of literary masters. This is an enduring memory I have of Virginia: a student has just finished reading her story, and Virginia, her eyes lit bright with the fires of genius, speaks intently to her about one of the characters in her story: 'The girl standing in the doorway— what color are her eyes? Are they downcast? Is she crying? What is she feeling? What's going to happen to her? I want to know more—write more, write more! Tell the whole story. I can't wait to read it!'"[3]

As for the tools with which Hamilton wrote, she worked to stay ahead of technology. First, she switched to an Adler, an expensive and high-end German typewriter with many special features. And then, when early word processors came on the market, she and Adoff invested in an IBM Displaywrite before many people had real personal computers for the home. Clunky by today's standards, the Displaywrite was the most advanced machine money could buy at the time. Its correction feature was revolutionary. In the past, a mistake meant a writer had to use messy correction tape or fluid, or retype a whole page. Hamilton figured that writing on a machine with memory and auto-correction would literally give her four extra months of living each year. Eventually, she and Adoff switched to high-end Dell computers with huge memory banks and Trinitron screens.

Some of Hamilton's finest books appeared after she mastered high-tech writing: *Drylongso* (1992), about a family's struggle against nature and the help of a dowser, or "water witch"; *Cousins* (1990), a story about family rivalry with a drowning at its center; and the much-honored *Her Stories: African American Folktales, Fairytales, and True Tales* (1995), Hamilton's all-female collection of tall tales and true stories. (For a selected list of Virginia Hamilton's published books and awards, see pages 89–94).

In 1992, Hamilton received a prize that outshone all the others. Among children's writers, the Hans Christian Andersen Medal is still thought to be the highest honor in the world. Awarded every other year, it recognizes an author's entire body of work. Queen Margrethe II of Denmark served as patron of the prize, which is sometimes referred to as the Little Nobel Award. The International Board on Books for Young People, or IBBY, chose the winner. Only four Americans—writers Meindert DeJong, Scott O'Dell, and Paula Fox, and illustrator Maurice Sendak—had won the Andersen Medal before Hamilton. Though she was thrilled, she quickly turned her attention to completing *Plain City*, a novel she published with Blue Sky/Scholastic in 1993.

In 1994, the Virginia Hamilton Conference at Kent State University, which began very simply as the Virginia Hamilton Lecture, celebrated its tenth anniversary. There, Hamilton received a letter of congratulations from Bill Clinton, the president of the United States, which she considered a high honor for any American citizen. She was especially pleased that the president and First Lady Hillary Clinton, whom she knew, had read a number of her books. This message has been preserved in the Virginia Hamilton archives at Kent State University for interested scholars to see in the future.

Dear Virginia:

I am delighted to congratulate you as you are honored by your friends, colleagues, and admirers at the tenth annual Virginia Hamilton Conference at Kent State University.

Throughout your distinguished literary career, you have been an eloquent voice for the excluded and dispossessed of America. Your magical prose has earned you a reputation around the world as one of the finest writers of children's literature of our time. Expanding the minds of millions of young readers, you have taught them invaluable lessons of the suffering and joy, of the fear and hope that all people share.

I am pleased to commend you for your tremendous achievements as a writer. You have contributed much to the cultural diversity that is one of our nation's greatest strengths, and I join young people everywhere in looking forward to enjoying your wonderful work in the years to come.

Hillary and I extend best wishes for every future happiness.

Sincerely,

Bill Clinton

It is not widely known, but Hamilton also was recognized by an earlier first lady, this one a Republican. Barbara Bush, wife of the first President Bush and mother of President George W. Bush, enjoyed Hamilton's writing and asked permission to read some of her work aloud in a RIF (Reading Is Fundamental) program. Mrs. Bush had one of her secretaries call Hamilton to say that the first lady wasn't comfortable dropping the endings of words, as Hamilton had written them. Would the author mind if she read the word endings her own way? Hamilton agreed, saying, "Tell Mrs. Bush she is welcome to read my books any way she likes." Later, when Hamilton received an invitation to visit the Bush White House, some of her Democratic friends asked why she would want to go, since she disagreed with a number of the then-president's policies. She waved their concerns away. "That's not his house," she reminded them. "That's my house."[4] Despite their different views, Hamilton respected the office President Bush held and liked that Mrs. Bush had featured her work in an RIF story hour, bringing it to the attention of many new readers.

It must, in those days, have seemed as if Hamilton were on top of the world. She was successful and honored by both Republican and Democratic first families. She had been awarded honorary Doctor of Humane Letters degrees from the Bank Street College of Education, OSU, and Wright State University, and in 1997, she would receive yet another one from Kent State University.

All was not as it seemed, though, for in private, Hamilton was battling breast cancer. When she was first diagnosed, advances had not yet been made in gene therapy and other cutting-edge treatments. Even ten years ago, many women fully recovered from this disease, however. Hamilton expected to be one of the lucky ones. She went into remission and her doctor joked that he didn't want to see her again, except at book signings. Instead of cutting back on work, as others might have done, she kept up her book-per-year pace.

She did, however, make it a point to begin traveling for pleasure and resting a bit more. Two places she and Adoff especially enjoyed were Florida and Puerto Rico, where they walked beside the ocean and read books they themselves hadn't written, for a change. On vacation, Hamilton enjoyed an Elmore Leonard mystery or even a glossy beach novel that let her empty her tired mind and recharge for her next project.

In 1995, Hamilton received another tremendous surprise. The MacArthur Foundation gave generous "genius grants" each year to the most creative people they could find. How these grants were awarded was a well-kept secret. No one knew who chose the MacArthur "geniuses" or decided just how much their winnings should be. The largest prize was $350,000, with no strings attached, and Hamilton received that amount, the most anyone won during her award year. Her first impulse, she said, was to help her two children become established in their artistic careers.

Leigh had by then become an opera singer, as Hamilton expected she might. She performed with a number of companies, mastered soprano roles in Mozart, and finally moved to Germany to marry and continue her career in classical music. Jaime kept his band going in New York for a number of years, but then left music behind to join the family business of writing. Very quickly, he received offers on five books. Adoff acted as his son's agent in these sales.

In November 1996, a journey to South Africa as part of the Citizen Ambassadors' Program's Children's Literature Delegation, was a high point of Hamilton's life. People to People International, the trip sponsors, believed that if natives of different countries had contact with one another, there would greater peace in the world. Hamilton's great idol, William Faulkner, had been a People to People ambassador, so she knew what an honor it was to be invited on a trip. She was invited to join the delegation, which included academics, critics, writers, and publishers—all of whom were children's literature specialists. Their goal was to strengthen ties among professionals who were involved in peace and understanding through children's books and reading. She visited Johannesburg/Pretoria, Soweto, Cape Town, and

Kruger National Park, where wild animals roamed freely in nature. Upon her return home, she recalled the two-week journey as being wonderful.

Hamilton's remaining years were filled with more travel, more tributes, and always more writing. In 1997, she had the satisfaction of seeing *Many Thousand Gone: African Americans from Slavery to Freedom* released in braille so that blind children might enjoy it.

By now, she had no financial worries. Nearly all of her books were still in print and selling steadily. Adoff negotiated a special arrangement with her new publisher, Scholastic, that meant she would be well taken care of in the future. Jean L. Feiwel, publisher, Children's Book Publishing and Distribution at Scholastic, was an important supporter in Hamilton's last years. Bonnie Verburg, her Scholastic editor, flew to Ohio so they could sit together beside a crackling fire and review pages while sipping the hot coffee Adoff brewed for them. When Hamilton's cancer recurred, she chose to keep working, and she wrote until the end of her life.

Always intrigued by the future, Hamilton was one of the very first authors to build an interactive Web site when that was a brand-new thing to do.

An America Online Member's Award-winner, she offered a choice of jokes, pictures of her beloved frog collection, snapshots of her family, and links to what she called "fun stuff" on her site. To young readers it also offers friendship, for there, Virginia Hamilton is still smiling on every page, making a warm personal connection with anyone who drops by. Its URL address is www.virginiahamilton.com, and she wanted readers to be able to visit even after her death. Her family plans to keep virginiahamilton.com online forever.

It wouldn't be Hamilton's site without a list of her wonderful books. They are all there, and they make visitors think of the author as a young, gutsy girl, moving to New York City to try to be a writer and somehow pulling it off exactly as she dreamed.

It seems hard to believe that before her true work began, there were so few books about African American families. How she managed to fill this gap, and to fill it so well, is as much a "telling," in its way, as the account of her grandfather's escape from slavery. His audience was small and Virginia Hamilton's remains large, but because of her, he will live on in the minds of thousands. His proud example will never be lost. And his unique story, like all the other stories she worked to preserve, will endure for as long as there continue to be words and curious people to read them.

Timeline

March 12, 1936 Virginia Hamilton is born in Yellow Springs, Ohio, to Etta Belle Perry Hamilton and Kenneth James Hamilton.

1952–1955 Hamilton attends Antioch College, Yellow Springs, Ohio.

1957–1958 Hamilton attends Ohio State University, Columbus, Ohio.

1958–1959 Hamilton moves to New York City. She attends the New School for Social Research.

March 19, 1960 Virginia Hamilton marries Arnold Adoff, an anthologist and poet.

1965 Hamilton and Adoff travel to the south of France.

1967 Hamilton publishes her first book, *Zeely*, with Macmillan Publishers.

1969 *The House of Dies Drear* receives the Mystery Writers of America's Edgar Allan Poe Award.

1974 *M. C. Higgins, the Great* receives the *Boston Globe/Horn Book* Citation.

1975 Hamilton is the first African American to win the Newbery Medal (for *M. C. Higgins, the Great,* published in 1974) and the National Book Award.

1990 Hamilton receives a Doctorate of Humane Letters from the Bank Street College of Education and the Regina Medal for Lifetime Achievement from the Catholic Library Association.

1992 Hamilton wins the Hans Christian Andersen Award, the highest honor in the world for a children's author.

1994 Hamilton receives a Doctorate of Humane Letters from Ohio State University. Kent State University marks the tenth anniversary of its Virginia Hamilton Conference.

1995 Hamilton is the first (and only) youth author to receive a MacArthur Foundation "genius grant." Hamilton receives a Doctorate of Humane Letters from Wright State University.

1997 Hamilton receives a Doctorate of Humane Letters from Kent State University.

February 19, 2002 Hamilton dies in Dayton, Ohio.

Selected
Reviews from
School Library
Journal

The Magical Adventures of Pretty Pearl
April 1983

Gr. 6 Up—In a blend of fantasy, folklore, realism and even aspects of her own family history, Hamilton tells an allegorical story of black people through the late Nineteenth Century. Pretty Pearl, a god child moved by the suffering of the captured slaves in Africa, comes down from on high on Mount Kenya with her powerful god brother, John de Conquer. Disguised as albatrosses, the gods travel with the slave ships to Georgia and lie low in southern soil for hundreds of years. Then, at the time of Reconstruction, Pretty Pearl goes among the people, armed with magic powers and powerful ancient spirits, but disguised as a human. She resides with the "inside folks," a self-sufficient community of fugitives from racism, who secretly live deep in the forests of southern Georgia, closely in touch with a remnant Cherokee band. Then, with the railroads and hunters coming nearer, the time comes for the people to leave their secret place: led by the Indians, they avoid the Ku Klux Klan strongholds and cross the Jordan to settle in Ohio. John Henry is Pretty Pearl's brother, a black giant spirit, wonderfully drawn as a laughing daredevil character who cannot help choosing the human way and will die challenging the machine. Like her brother, Pretty Pearl loses her magic power and becomes part of the human community—which grows strong with the spirits of the ancient gods among the people with the power of their stories. This imaginative truth of enduring community is perfectly expressed in Hamilton's style, which moves from simple narrative to folk-knowledge of "nut, leaf and bark," to colloquial idiom and blues rhythms; her telling demonstrates that songs, tales and changes are rooted in the daily experience of "folks everywhere," and that language is a living force. —Hazel Rochman, High School Library, University of Chicago Laboratory Schools

Sweet Whispers, Brother Rush
September 1982

Gr. 7–10—With her father long gone and M'Vy, her practical nurse mother, away most of the time, fourteen-year-old Teresa (Tree) cares for her retarded older brother, Dab. In her loneliness and awakening sexuality she sees the handsome ghost of her dead uncle, Brother Rush, who takes her back to several scenes of her early childhood, where she discovers tragic family secrets. These dramatic vignettes of past anguish intensify the powerful center of the book, which is Tree's tender mothering relationship with her brother and her raging grief as he dies from the hereditary blood disease porphyria. Like Buddy in *The Planet of Junior Brown* (Macmillan, 1971), Tree is one of the responsible kids "who stay and hold down everythang." But, strong as she is, she is full of anger, troubled about growing up, self-conscious about her body, even about being black. As she begins to cope with her ambivalent feelings, she feels compassion for those she had once seen as outcast—the old bag lady, her own deserting father. Finally, she is able to accept her mother's great love for her, even while they both must face that M'Vy had never been able to love Dab: "I beat him, help me, I beat him." Poetic, many-layered, yet not difficult to read, this is Hamilton at her best, with a humane acceptance of people in their struggle, and hope for the power of their love. —Hazel Rochman, High School Library, University of Chicago Laboratory Schools

Willie Bea and the Time the Martians Landed
December 1983

Gr. 5–8—"Awful funny" is how twelve-year-old Willie Bea sums up the Halloween happenings in this warm story of family love and the strength such love gives a young girl on her own adventurous journey. It is a special Sunday near the end of harvest time in 1938 and Willie Bea's large extended family is gathered in her grandparents' homestead in Ohio for a Halloween feast. The security in the "Sunday-cooking house" makes deliciously scary the thought of later trick-or-treating in the Gobble-un haunted dark. But even in daylight, monsters are not what they seem: Willie Bea's overgrown awkward boy-cousin, Big, is punished for wrongdoing, though she knows that he means no harm and she bickers with his sister. Then, after dinner, this eloquent but slow-moving story of love and family relationships picks up speed. The Orson Welles trick broadcast of *War of the Worlds* sends the family, like much of the country, into panic. Willie Bea steals away to investigate the invaders that have landed on a nearby farm—in her Halloween hobo-wanderer costume, striding like a giant on her stilts through the still dark world. The space monsters she sees with their glaring evil eyes turn out to be the new combine-harvesters, and the voice she hears in their roaring noise, telling her to "come home," is really Big's. The next day, her father gently makes her face these "facts"; but her beloved fortune-telling aunt holds her to the truth of the strange and unknown. Hamilton moves with ease from farce (in the adults' hysteria, a small child asks, "Where's the end of the world? . . . I wanta see it."), to sudden dread; from heart-catching scenes of physical and verbal affection to candor about the complications of love (even while she adores her mother, sometimes Willie Bea, ashamed, longs to be her aunt's child). All the characters are strongly individualized, complex, surprising. —Hazel Rochman, High School Library, University of Chicago Laboratory Schools

Arilla Sun Down
October 1976

Gr. 8–10—In an unusual, colorful, and sometimes confusing combination of black, Indian, and teenage parlance, twelve-year-old Arilla Adams tells of coming to terms with her strange and unpredictable family. Her mother, who is black, is warm and protective; her father, half-Indian/half-black, is prone to leaving home when the spirit moves him; and, her sixteen-year-old brother envisions himself an Indian militant. At the story's end, she proves herself to her father and brother (changing her name from Arilla Running Moon to Arilla Sun Down—Moon is passive, Sun is active). Aside from the structural and language complexity (stream-of-consciousness prose mixing verbless sentences and participal phrases), Arilla's feelings and thoughts are not at all typical of twelve-year-olds. Nonetheless, very memorable and moving scenes from the story lodge in readers' minds, and this is as compelling if even more demanding reading that Hamilton's *M. C. Higgins, the Great* (Macmillan, 1974). —Jack Forman, Eastern Massachusetts Regional Library System, Boston

Plain City
November 1993

Gr. 6–8—Discovering that her mother and relatives lied about her father dying in Vietnam, angry Buhlaire-Marie Sims, twelve, is determined to find and communicate with her dad. When he rescues her during a January blizzard, he leads his daughter to a highway underpass, his space among the homeless of Plain City. Buhlaire learns that her father is a troubled man, estranged from his family because of his mental instability and racially mixed parentage. Although he treats her kindly, she begins to perceive the confusion and unpredictability of his life. Buhlaire has experienced her own ostracization because of her mother's nightclub career, her home among the stilted river bottom "water houses," and her light skin. Although she is loved and cared for, her adolescent sensibilities are aroused when she realizes that her family has shielded her from her own identity. Through candid thoughts, realistic dialogue, and a symbolic blend of setting and self-discovery, Hamilton has created a testimonial on the powerful bonds of blood and "back time," or heritage. Buhlaire emerges from her emotional turmoil and quest with an appreciation for the attentions and personal struggles of a classmate; with renewed affection for her family; and, with a compassionate understanding of hard choices that are part of life. —Gerry Larson, Chewning Junior High School, Durham, North Carolina

Bluish
November 1999

Gr. 5–8— Ten-year-old Dreenie, a recent transfer to a New York City magnet school, is fascinated with her fellow classmate, Natalie, a girl battling leukemia. Kids call her Bluish, not a derogatory term for her black and Jewish heritage, "Blewish," but because of the effects of chemotherapy on her skin. Dreenie's other friend, Tuli, is a flamboyant girl who is looking for the stability and normalcy that Dreenie and her family have. Through four weeks in December, these three girls move into a closer circle of friendship, with alternating feelings of fear, generosity, and kindness. Together, they are able to reach out to the rest of the class in accepting and celebrating Bluish as she is. Though her future is uncertain—it will take five years of remission before any assurance—readers are left seeing curly copper hair hiding under her skullcap, delighting her friends and inspiring hope. The narration alternates between Dreenie's journal and a third-person narrator, allowing readers to glimpse the firsthand incredulity of a child witnessing serious illness and also the reaction of a classroom community as it follows the highs and lows of Bluish's health. This structure doesn't always work, and readers may be puzzled when the narrative voice switches from third person to include Dreenie's journal entries. Hamilton occasionally slips into a heavy-handed adult perspective that does not reflect a ten-year-old's experience. At times, topics are introduced but are never fleshed out, such as Tuli's capricious living situation or Dreenie's sister's accusation that Dreenie "sure ain't one of us Anneva and Gerald Browns." A sensitive and quiet story that is not fully realized. —Katie O'Dell Madison, Multnomah County Library, Portland, Oregon

In the Beginning: Creation Stories from Around the World
December 1988

Gr. 6 Up—Twenty-five creation myths from such diverse cultures as China, Tahiti, Micronesia, and Australia. Illustrated with forty-two dramatic, full-color paintings, this is a handsome representative collection. Hamilton's introduction briefly defines creation myths and places them within the formal cultural structure that gives them authority. Her commitment to stay true to the simplicity of style of many creation myths results in some brilliant retellings, complete with the clarity of vision and fluidity of language synonymous with her work. While most of these retold myths are highly successful, others lack the precision of the "perfect word" associated with Hamilton. (One example is the jarring use of the modern word "aide," as in aides to a god in a Zambian creation myth.) Although the placement of the explanatory notes at the end of each myth is less effective than if they were placed at the beginning, the book is handsomely designed. Each myth opens with a striking full-page painting, each of which is truly evocative and powerful in design and content. Text and illustrations together result in a strong, effective piece of work. —Janice M. Del Negro, Chicago Public Library

A White Romance
January 1988

Gr. 8 Up—Hamilton's novel works on at least five levels: within the personality of the protagonist, within her immediate circle, within her setting of school and neighborhood, between her world and the intrusive white world, and between the novel and the reader, especially if that reader is unfamiliar with the details of black urban American life. Talley's formerly all-black high school has been converted to an integrated magnet school for the entire district. This means an influx of white students. The culture shock is immediate and prolonged. Add to the mix drugs, heavy metal rock, Talley's struggles to establish her own values, and an almost unbearable level of adolescent sexual tension, and you have a very potent brew indeed. Talley and her circle of friends are effectively portrayed: Didi, her white best friend, hopelessly involved with Roady, who is crippled both in mind and body through drug use; David, his dealer, who now has his eye on Talley; and Victor, who is attempting to save her from her fixation on David. The setting of school corridors, city streets, and a rock concert right out of Hieronymous Bosch is equally real. The use of black English throughout may be a challenge to some readers, but is well worth the effort, since the book would be weakened in any other idiom. Not a happy book, but a vivid, even surrealistic and insightful depiction of painful relationships. —Barbara Hutcheson, Greater Victoria Public Library, British Columbia

A Little Love
October 1984

Gr. 6–9—Hamilton unfolds her character, a young black woman with many problems, through a narrative filled with a mixture of difficult and unfamiliar street jargon and black English.

Seventeen-year-old Sheema Hadley, half child, half woman, has never known her mother, who died in childbirth, or her father, who abandoned her as an infant. Her grandparents, who are approaching senility, have always cared for her. Sexually active and street-wise, Sheema feels unloved, despises her obesity and fears "The Bomb" in particular and the world in general. She derives comfort from food and her "cook," understanding boyfriend, Forest, who eventually asks her to marry him. Sheema's character is drawn through her inner thoughts—she broods about school, the responsibility of caring for her elderly, often recalcitrant, grandparents and her absent father. Eventually Granmom tells Sheema just enough details about her father to enable her to piece bits together and convince Forrest to help her search for him—a search that ends successfully but not happily after only two days. But Sheema, who learns that she must face adult problems, begins to mature. Readers who get beyond Hamilton's idiosyncratic use of language will find universal problems in this story of family relationships and emotional conflicts. But too many issues cloud the story, and less patient readers may not be willing to dwell on Sheema's problems long enough to finish the book. —Bertha Cheatham

The Dark Way
December 1990

Gr. 5 Up—Twenty-five eerie tales from folklore, myth, and legend told around the world, written with resonance and precision. Presented for readers' shivery enjoyment are stories ancient and modern, myth and fable, some playful and many truly horrifying. Some of the characters are motivated by the fear of death or the desire to make harmony in their worlds. But here too are the familiar folklore catalysts of jealousy, greed, curiosity, and disobedience. Of course, there are also poor, hapless souls who just by virtue of happenstance fall victim to evil-doers. Most effective are the tales from folklore that lack the distant, formal quality of some of the myths and legends. And those stories with children as protagonists strike the most affecting chord. Even without illustrations, these tales are chilling. But add to them Davis's disquieting portraits, and the stories really pack a wallop. Frightening is the depiction of an oni as it screams in pain from a sword plunged into its tongue. Conversely, there is almost a peaceful, pink-cheeked quietness to the portrait of a dying priest as his soul leaves his body in the form of a butterfly. These stories are ripe for telling, and both readers and tellers will find useful the background notes and comments at the end of each story. Read and enjoy. But beware, for there are witches in the air. —Denia Lewis Hester, Dewey School, Evanston, Illinois

Second Cousins
November 1988

Gr. 5–8—In the first few chapters of this sequel to Hamilton's *Cousins* (Philomel, 1990), Cammy Coleman is still reacting emotionally to the tragic drowning death the previous summer of her close cousin Patty Ann. This summer's big event is the family reunion, with cousins, second cousins, third cousins, and more coming from far and wide to Cammy's small town. After a rocky start, she forms a special friendship with Jahnina, also known as Fractal, who is from New York City. (The various characters all seem to have one or more nicknames, which may create some confusion for readers.) As the girls get to know one another better and better, however, Cammy is unable to accept the true nature of their relationship—they are half sisters. Through dialect and believable actions and outcomes, Hamilton's characters spring to life. Punchy sentence fragments accurately reflect the rush of emotion felt by preadolescents as they are inevitably introduced to the complications of adulthood and family dynamics. Although the plot is thin and the tone somewhat uneven, the emotional truths are both dramatic and real. Hamilton's fans and those interested in the joys and heartaches of growing up will enjoy the extended Coleman family. —Peg Solonika, Carnegie Library of Pittsburgh, Pennsylvania

List of Selected Works

The All Jahdu Storybook, Harcourt, 1991.
Anthony Burns: The Defeat and Triumph of a Fugitive Slave, Knopf, 1988.
Arilla Sun Down, Greenwillow, 1976.
The Bells of Christmas, Harcourt, 1989.
Bluish, Scholastic, 2002.
Cousins, Putnam, 1990.
The Dark Way: Stories from the Spirit World, Harcourt, 1990.
Drylongso, Harcourt Brace Jovanovich, 1992.
Dustland, Greenwillow, 1980.
The Gathering, Greenwillow, 1981.
The Girl Who Spun Gold, Scholastic, 2000.
Her Stories: African American Folktales, Fairytales, and True Tales, Scholastic, 1995.
The House of Dies Drear, Macmillan, 1968.

*In the Beginning: Creation Stories from Around
   the World*, Harcourt, 1988.
Jaguarundi, Blue Sky Press, 1995.
Jahdu, Greenwillow, 1980.
Junius Over Far, Harper & Row, 1985.
Justice and Her Brothers, Greenwillow, 1978.
A Little Love, Philomel, 1984.
The Magical Adventures of Pretty Pearl,
   Harper, 1983.
*Many Thousand Gone: African Americans from
   Slavery to Freedom*, Knopf, 1992.
M. C. Higgins, the Great, Macmillan, 1974.
*The Mystery of Drear House: The Conclusion of
   the Dies Drear Chronicle*, Greenwillow, 1987.
The People Could Fly: American Black Folktales,
   Knopf, 1985.
Plain City, Blue Sky, Scholastic. 1993.
The Planet of Junior Brown, Macmillan, 1971.
*A Ring of Tricksters: Animal Tales from
   America, the West Indies, and Africa*, Blue
   Sky Press, 1997.
*Paul Robeson: The Life and Times of a Free Black
   Man*, Harper & Row, 1974.
Second Cousins, Scholastic, 1998.
Sweet Whispers, Brother Rush, Philomel, 1982.
Time-Ago Lost: More Tales of Jahdu,
   Macmillan, 1973.

The Time-Ago Tales of Jadhu, Macmillan, 1969.

Time Pieces: The Book of Times, Scholastic, 2002.

W. E .B. DuBois: A Biography, Ty Crowell Company, 1972.

Wee Winnie Witch's Skinny: An Original Scare Tale for Halloween, Scholastic, 2002.

When Birds Could Talk and Bats Could Sing: The Adventures of Bruh Sparrow, Sis Wren, and Their Friends, Blue Sky Press, 1995.

A White Romance, Philomel, 1987.

Willie Bea and the Time the Martians Landed, Greenwillow, 1983.

Zeely, Macmillan, 1967.

List of Selected Awards

Doctor of Humane Letters, Bank Street College of Education (1990)

Doctor of Humane Letters, Kent State University (1997)

Doctor of Humane Letters, Ohio State University (1994)

Doctor of Humane Letters, Wright State University (1995)

Hans Christian Andersen Award (1992)

Laura Ingalls Wilder Award (1995)

***Anthony Burns: The Defeat and Triumph of a Fugitive Slave* (1988)**

Boston Globe/Horn Book Award for Nonfiction (1988)

Jane Addams Children's Book Award (1989)

***Cousins* (1990)**

New York Public Library 100 Titles for Reading and Sharing (2001)

***Her Stories: African American Folktales, Fairy Tales and True Tales* (1995)**

Hungry Mind Review Children's Book of Distinction (1996)

***The House of Dies Drear* (1968)**

Edgar Allan Poe Award ("The Edgar"), Mystery Writers of America, Inc. (1969)

***In the Beginning: Creation Stories from Around the World* (1988)**

The Horn Book Fanfare Selection (1985)
Parents Magazine, Best Books of the Year (1998)
Time Magazine, One of the 12 Best Books for Young Readers (1988)

***A Little Love* (1984)**

Coretta Scott King Award (1985)

***The Magical Adventures of Pretty Pearl* (1983)**

American Library Association Best Book for Young Adults (1983)

***M. C. Higgins, the Great* (1974)**

Boston Globe/Horn Book Award for Fiction (1974)
National Book Award (1975)
Lewis Carroll Shelf Award (1976)
Newbery Medal (1974)

***The People Could Fly: American Black Folktales* (1985)**

Coretta Scott King Award (1986)

***Sweet Whispers, Brother Rush* (1982)**

American Library Association Best Book for Young Adults (1983)

Boston Globe/Horn Book Award for Fiction (1983)
Coretta Scott King Award (1983)
Library of Congress Best Books for Children (1982)

When Birds Could Talk and Bats Could Sing (1995)

Publisher's Weekly Best Books (1996)

Glossary

abolitionist One who fights against slavery.

accountant One whose job it is to keep track of tax and business records.

alma mater The Latin name for the college or university one attended.

anthologist An editor who selects short literary works to preserve in a book.

assassination The act of murdering an important person, usually a political leader.

aura A feeling, an atmosphere.

bassist A musician who plays the bass.

biography The story of one's life.

bondage Slavery.

citation To receive recognition for something.

compelling Forceful, or strong.

conventional Customary, standard

coveted Greatly desired.

crossbeam A ceiling plank stretched from one wall to another.

cyclone A violent storm.

delegation An official group.

discontent Unhappiness.

dormitory A college or university residence hall.

eccentric Unusual.

flourished When something has grown easily.

forsythia A flowering plant.

fugitive A refugee who flees or leaves where he or she is from originally.

ginseng The root of an herb that possesses beneficial qualities.

Great Depression The term used to describe the era of joblessness and poverty that occurred in the United States after the stock market crash of 1929.

immigrants Non-natives, or new settlers who come from another country.

influential Important.

legitimate Authentic, genuine.

liberation Freedom.

lore Folktales, stories.

MacArthur Grant A large cash prize that is awarded by the Chicago-based John D. and Catherine T. MacArthur Foundation Fellowship Awards to "geniuses" who create exceptional work. Recipients are free to use the award money any way they wish. In 1995, Virginia Hamilton was awarded a $350,000 grant.

mandolin A stringed musical instrument.

monotonous Boring.

parallel Extending in the same direction but not touching.

prestigious Distinguished.

racism Bigotry against a different racial or ethnic group.

remission Retreat, cure.

repercussions Impacts.

sentinel A person or animal who guards a group against surprise.

silo An airtight tower for preserving grain.

spectacle Sight, vision.

strip mining Mining with no care for the environment.

telekinetic Having the ability to move things without touching them.

telepathic Having the ability to communicate through thoughts

thriving Growing easily.

tolerant Broad minded.

traumatic Describing something that is shocking and painful

ultimate Greatest.

valedictorian Top graduate of a class.

wattles Flesh pieces that hang from a bird's chin.

Watusi A cattle-raising people who mostly live in Burundi and Rwanda in Africa.

whimsical Amusing.

For More Information

Due to the changing nature of Internet links, the Rosen Publishing Group, Inc., has developed an online list of Web sites related to the subject of this book. This site is updated regularly. Please use this link to access the list:

http://www.rosenlinks.com/lab/vham/

For Further Reading

Apseloff, Marilyn F. "Virginia Hamilton."
    Dictionary of Literary Biography:
    American Writers for Children Since 1960.
    Vol. 52. Detroit: Gale Research, 1999.
Mangal, Melina. *Virginia Hamilton*. Boston:
    Mitchell Lane Publishers, 2002.
Mikkelson, Nina. *Virginia Hamilton*.
    Toronto, ON: Twayne Publishers, 1994.
Wheeler, Jill. *Virginia Hamilton*. Edina, MN:
    Abdo Publishing Company, 1997.

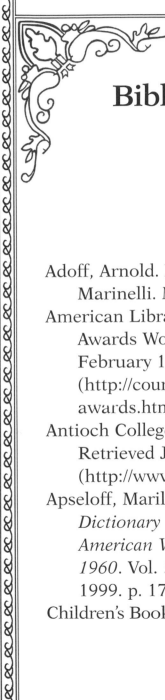

Bibliography

Adoff, Arnold. Interview with Deborah Marinelli. March 7, 2002.

American Library Association. "Book Awards Worth Knowing." Retrieved February 18, 2002 (http://courses.wcupa.edu.johnson/ awards.html).

Antioch College. "About the College." Retrieved January 11, 2002 (http://www.antioch-college.edu).

Apseloff, Marilyn F. "Virginia Hamilton." *Dictionary of Literary Biography: American Writers for Children Since 1960*. Vol. 52. Detroit: Gale Research, 1999. p. 174.

Children's Book Council. "Virginia Hamilton."

Retrieved January 7, 2002
(http://www.cbcbooks.org/html/
virginia_hamilton.html).

Ferguson, Sue. Administrator, Stuvesant High School. Interview with Deborah Marinelli. March 2, 2002.

Hamilton, Virginia. "About Virginia Hamilton." Marketing brochure. Scholastic Press, Inc. Blue Sky Imprint. Virginia Hamilton Papers, Kent State University Archives, Box 1.

Hamilton, Virginia. "Planting Seeds." *Horn Book Magazine*. November/December 1992, pp. 674–675.

Hartill, Lane. "A Brief History of Interracial Marriage." *Christian Science Monitor*. July 25, 2001. Retrieved March 7, 2002 (http://www.csmonitor.com/durable/2001/07/25/p15sl.htm).

H. W. Wilson/Educational Paperback Association. "Arnold Adoff." January 6, 2002. Retrieved February 3, 2002 (http://www.webspirs.cgi?sp.usernumber.p=570740&url=yes&sp.nextform=show1rec.htm).

H. W. Wilson/Educational Paperback Association. "Virginia Hamilton." Retrieved February 1, 2002 (http://www.edupaperback.org/authorbios/Hamilton_Virginia).

Jackson, Dick. Interview with Deborah
    Marinelli. March 4, 2002.

Mikkelsen, Nina. *Virginia Hamilton*. New York:
    Twayne's United States Authors Series, 1994.

Miller, Nolan. Interview with Deborah
    Marinelli. February 28, 2002.

Moss, Meredith. "Storyteller." *Dayton Daily
    News*, August 7, 1994, p. E-1.

Richardson, Dale. "The Children, The Newbery,
    and Virginia Hamilton." *RAP Dayton*.
    March 1975, p. 11.

Wallis, Don. "In Memorium." *Yellow Springs
    News*, March 6, 2002.

Wilsonweb Biographies Plus, *Fourth Book of
    Junior Authors and Illustrators*, H. W.
    Wilson Company, 1999 update.

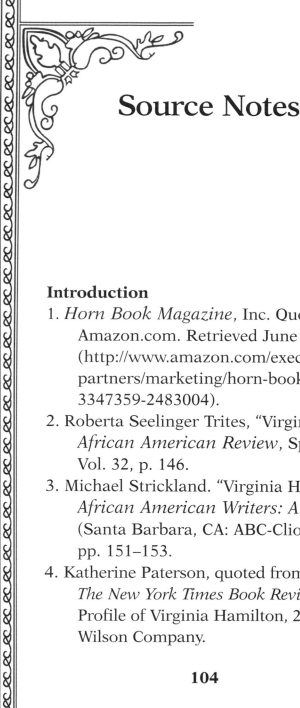

Source Notes

Introduction

1. *Horn Book Magazine,* Inc. Quoted on Amazon.com. Retrieved June 1, 2002 (http://www.amazon.com/exec/obidos/subst/partners/marketing/horn-book.html/103-3347359-2483004).

2. Roberta Seelinger Trites, "Virginia Hamilton," *African American Review,* Spring 1998, Vol. 32, p. 146.

3. Michael Strickland. "Virginia Hamilton." *African American Writers: A Dictionary.* (Santa Barbara, CA: ABC-Clio, Inc., 2000), pp. 151–153.

4. Katherine Paterson, quoted from her article in *The New York Times Book Review.* (NDG) in Profile of Virginia Hamilton, 2000, H. W. Wilson Company.

5. Nolan Miller. Interview with Deborah Marinelli. February 28, 2002.

Chapter 1

1. Virginia Hamilton, "Planting Seeds," *Horn Book Magazine*, November/December 1992, p. 674.

2. Rudine Sims Bishop. "An Appreciation of Virginia Hamilton," *Horn Book Magazine*, Vol. 71, No. 4, August 1995, pp. 442–444.

3. Virginia Hamilton, "Here's How It Goes: A Tale-Teller's Tale," *National Council of Teachers of English ALAN Review*, Spring 1979, Vol. 6, No. 3, p. 1.

4. Ibid.

5. Pam Cottrel, "Hometown Influenced Her Writing," *Dayton Daily News*, February 15, 1995, p. Z6–1

6. Diane Chiddister, "Stories of Courage and Spirit," *Yellow Springs News*, November 30, 1995, Vol. 116, No. 48, p. 8.

7. Meredith Moss, "Storyteller," *Dayton Daily News*, August 7, 1994.

8. Virginia Hamilton, "Changing Woman Working." 1981, pp. 54–55, Archives and Special Collections of Kent State University, Virginia Hamilton Papers, Box 1.

9. Rudine Sims Bishop, "An Appreciation of Virginia Hamilton," *Horn Book Magazine*, Vol. 71, No. 4, August 1995, pp. 442–444.

10. Ibid., pp. 442–444.

11. Virginia Hamilton, "Worlds of My Own." *Once Upon a Time: In Honor of the Twentieth Anniversary of Reading Is Fundamental* (New York: G. P. Putnam's Sons, 1986), p. 58.
12. "Virginia Hamilton." Retrieved January 25, 2002 (http://www.wordmuseum.com/ virginiahamiltoninterview.htm).

Chapter 2
1. Nolan Miller. Interview with Deborah Marinelli. February 28, 2002.
2. Ibid.
3. Ibid.
4. Alice Demetrius Stock, "Hamilton Grew Up in House of Tales," *Pittsburgh Post Gazette*, February 26, 1997, p. D-6.
5. "Welcome to the Ohio State University." OSU. 2000. Retrieved February, 1, 2002 (http://www.acs.ohio-state.edu/ index_alt.php).
6. Greenville Public Library. "Juvenile Books Author of the Month." Retrieved January 7, 2002 (http://www.ultranet.com/~greenvil/ Childrens_Webpage).
7. Virginia Hamilton, "Planting Seeds," *Horn Book Magazine*, November/December 1992, p. 674.
8. Nina Mikkelsen, "A Conversation with Virginia Hamilton," *Journal of Youth Services in Libraries* 7, 1994, p. 382.

Chapter 3

1. H. W. Wilson/Educational Paperback Association. "Virginia Hamilton." 1999. Retrieved February 1, 2002 (http://www.edupaperback.org/ authorbios/Hamilton_Virginia.html).
2. Virginia Hamilton, "Planting Seeds," *Horn Book Magazine*, November/December 1992, pp. 674–674.
3. Dick Jackson. Interview with Deborah Marinelli. March 4, 2002.
4. Ibid.

Chapter 4

1. Virginia Hamilton, "About Virginia Hamilton," Marketing brochure, Scholastic Inc., Blue Sky Press Imprint. Virginia Hamilton Papers, Kent State University Archives, Box 1.
2. "Virginia Hamilton: My Biography." Scholastic.com. (http://teacher.scholastic.com/ writewit/diary/bio.htm).
3. Arnold Adoff. Interview with Deborah Marinelli. March 7, 2002.
4. Marilyn F. Apseloff, "Virginia Hamilton," *Dictionary of Literary Biography: American Writers for Children Since 1960*. (Detroit: Gale Research, 1999), Vol. 52, p. 174.
5. Carol Hurst's Children's Literature Site. Retrieved January 23, 2002 (http://www.carolhurst.com/ authors/vhamilton.html).

6. Dale Richardson, "The Children, the Newbery, and Virginia Hamilton," *RAP Dayton*, March 1975, p. 11, The Virginia Hamilton Papers, Kent State University Archives, Box 1.

Chapter 5

1. Virginia Hamilton, "Planting Seeds," *Horn Book Magazine*, November/December 1992, p. 674.
2. Don Wallis, "In Memorium," *Yellow Springs News*, March 6, 2002.
3. Ibid.
4. Arnold Adoff. Interview with Deborah Marinelli. March 7, 2002.

Index

About the Author
Deborah Marinelli holds a Ph.D in English from the State University of New York at Albany and an M.A. in liberal arts education from St. John's College, Sante Fe, New Mexico. A professional writer, researcher, and editor for twenty years, she has published fiction and nonfiction.

Photo Credits
Cover, p. 2 courtesy of Arnold Adoff and the Kent State University Virginia Hamilton Conference Foundation.

Series Design and Layout
Tahara Hasan

Editor
Annie Sommers

Acknowledgments
The author gratefully acknowledges the generous assistance of: Arnold Adoff, Dick Jackson, Nolan Miller, and Janet Schulman; Rachel Aydt, adjunct lecturer, New School for Social Research, New York City; Nancy Birk, curator of Special Collections & university archivist, Kent State University; Sue Ferguson, Stuyvesant High School, New York City; Cara Gilgenbach, associate curator, Special Collections & Archives, Kent State University Libraries; Suzanne Gourlie, *Yellow Springs News*; Susan Rogers, Kent State University; Sam Roshon, historical librarian, Columbus, Ohio; Michael Roudette, reference librarian, New York Public Library; Scott Sanders, Antioch College archivist; Laura Schulte-Cooper, Association for Library Service to Children, Chicago; and reference librarians of the Kinderhook Library in Kinderhook, New York, at Antioch College in Yellow Springs, Ohio, and at the East Greenbush Library in East Greenbush, New York.